To my little friend, Clara Scott-Jones, with love – P.E.

For my wonderful Willow – R.H.

First published in 2005 by Macmillan Children's Books
A division of Macmillan Publishers Limited
20 New Wharf Road, London N1 9RR
Basingstoke and Oxford
Associated companies throughout the world
www.panmacmillan.com

ISBN 0 333 96444 6 (HB)
ISBN 0 333 96445 4 (PB)

1 3 5 7 9 8 6 4 2 (HB)
1 3 5 7 9 8 6 4 2 (PB)

A CIP catalogue record for this book is available from the British Library.

Printed in China by Leo Paper Group

Catch that Kitten!

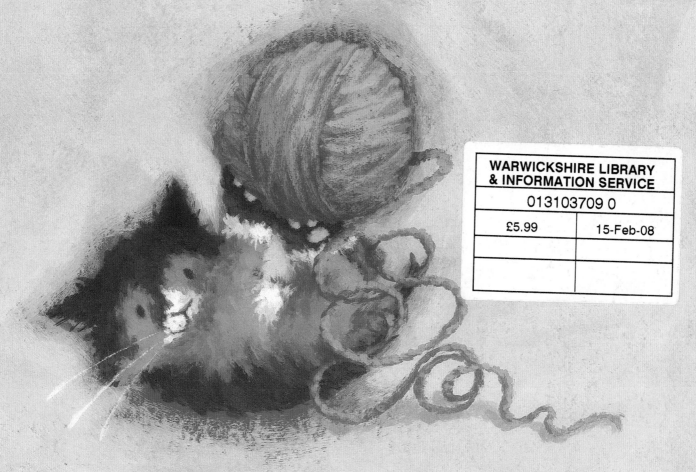

Pamela Duncan Edwards

illustrated by Rebecca Harry

MACMILLAN CHILDREN'S BOOKS

Tilly has five kittens in her basket.

One, two,

three,

four. . .

Uh-oh!

Where's Snowball?
Is he in the dolls' house?

No, Snowball is driving the train.
What a **clever** kitten!

Now Tilly has five kittens in her basket.

One,

two,

three,

four...

Uh-oh!

Where's Midnight?
Is Midnight driving the train, too?

No, Midnight is frightening the big dog.
What a **brave** kitten!

Now Tilly has five kittens in her basket.

One,

two,

three,

four...

Uh-oh!

Where's Ginger?
Is Ginger frightening the big dog, too?

No, Ginger is playing at dressing-up.

What a **funny** kitten!

Now Tilly has five kittens
in her basket.

One,

two,

three,

four . . .

Uh-oh!

Where's Boots?
Is Boots playing at dressing-up, too?

No, Boots is talking on the telephone.

What a **friendly** kitten!

Now Tilly has five kittens
in her basket.

One,

two,

three,

four...

Uh-oh!

Where's Pirate?
Is Pirate talking on the telephone, too?

No, Pirate is hiding in the dolls' house.
What a **silly** kitten!

Now Tilly has five kittens
in her basket.

One, two, three, four...

. . . five.

Good night! Sleep tight!

Uh-oh!

Also illustrated by Rebecca Harry:

Ruby Flew Too!

written by

Jonathan Emmett